Strength in Every Scar:

A Mother's C-Section Journey

ISBN-13: 978-1-964400-08-2

Designed by: Ruth Fleury

Printed in the United States of America

Dedication

This book is dedicated to all cesarean mothers, pregnant women, family and friends of a woman whose child delivery experience was via cesarean. Through sharing my story, I hope to offer encouragement to those facing unexpected challenges. In sharing my story, I hope to encourage other mothers facing unexpected challenges. Every birth experience is unique, and the bond formed in those moments is what truly matters.

Contents

Introduction

Have you ever heard the saying, "Once you have a C-section, you'll always have a C-section for childbirth?" That was my experience. As a first-time mom in 2009, it was incredibly scary. It had already been a long day at work, and after that, I headed to my prenatal checkup. The wait at the hospital seemed endless, and it felt like time was standing still.

Chapter One

Baby Joy

The First Journey

I was overjoyed when I found out I was pregnant. Although I wasn't sure what to expect during the pregnancy, I had some childcare experience that helped ease my nerves. I babysat my first niece when I was twelve, and I did a great job changing her diapers, feeding her, and helping her fall asleep. My first job at a daycare center in Canarsie, Brooklyn, further boosted my confidence in child-rearing.

Overall, I felt great during my first pregnancy. I didn't experience morning sickness or swollen feet. However, as I entered my third trimester, I became increasingly uncomfortable at night, struggling to find a comfortable position. I found myself switching sides or sitting up every few minutes. I attended all my prenatal visits, and my blood pressure remained normal throughout the pregnancy. The baby was developing well. At the time, I was in college and working part-time as a paraprofessional in a public school.

Then, on Friday, February 14, 2009, I had a prenatal visit, and that's when my life changed...

A Journey Through Preeclampsia

Facing the Unexpected

I had always envisioned my pregnancy as a time of joy and anticipation, a natural path toward motherhood. But as I entered my third trimester, my excitement was overshadowed by unease. A routine checkup revealed high blood pressure and the alarming diagnosis of preeclampsia.

The news hit me like a ton of bricks. I had spent months preparing for a calm, natural birth, but now my plans were at risk. The doctor explained that preeclampsia could lead to serious complications for both me and my baby, and that a cesarean section might be necessary. A flood of emotions, fear, confusion, and a deep sense of loss rushed over me as I grappled with the reality that my ideal birth experience was slipping away.

As my condition progressed, I found myself frequently being monitored. Each checkup was a new source of anxiety, but I clung to the support of my family and medical team. They reassured me that both my health and the baby's well-being were their top priorities. Yet, no matter how many times they said it, I couldn't shake the feeling that my dream of a natural birth was slipping away, replaced by something I hadn't anticipated.

The following day, the doctor decided it was time for delivery. Relief and terror washed over me in equal measure. I was given an epidural and instructed to crouch like a cat, arching my back for the procedure. My back was cleaned with a cold substance, and the sensation of being taped into place was uncomfortable. The needle of the epidural was thick, and I couldn't help but flinch, but I tried to team explained that a C-section was now the safest option, given my condition. I felt a strange mix of resignation and acceptance as I braced myself for the unexpected turn my birth story had taken.

My husband and mother couldn't join me in the operating room and had to wait anxiously in the waiting area. In that moment, I felt a rush of disbelief and emotion, alone in the sterile, bright room, with only the medical team to guide me through what was happening.

Once in the operating room, I was surrounded by a whirlwind of activity. The harsh lights and the array of sterile instruments were intimidating, but the calm professionalism of the staff helped ease my nerves. As the spinal block took effect, I felt a warm numbness slowly spread through my lower body, rendering me completely still. The surgery began, and though I felt pressure, there was no pain. I focused on my breathing, reminding myself that I was about to meet my baby. Moments later, the room was fi lled with the sound of a newborn's cry. Tears welled up in my eyes as the doctor announced the arrival of my son, Rufredo.

Unfortunately, I couldn't hold my baby right away due to medical complications. My body was shaking uncontrollably, and I felt a cold that pierced through me. My mother, concerned, requested a blanket for me, as the air conditioner was set too low in the labor and delivery unit. It wasn't until a few hours later, after the shaking had subsided, that I was moved to a recovery room. But even then, I didn't get to see my baby until the next day.

When I finally laid eyes on him, he was perfect, a tiny bundle of warmth and life. Despite the unexpected C-section, the love I felt for him was instant and all-encompassing, erasing any lingering disappointment from my changed birth plan.

Recovery, however, was another story. The physical pain from the surgery was intense, and managing my condition added an extra layer of diffi culty. Getting out of bed and walking was a challenge. I remember a relative visiting me at the hospital, trying to cheer me up with jokes. As I laughed, I suddenly felt a sharp pain, a staple from the incision came loose. The pain at the incision site was unbearable. I had to clutch my stomach and stand still for a few minutes, waiting for the agony to subside.

Though preeclampsia had led me down a difficult and unexpected path, it also brought me closer to my son and allowed me to discover a deep resilience within myself.

Through my C-section and the trials of preeclampsia, I found strength, love, and a profound sense of beauty in embracing the unexpected.

✨ My C-Section Recovery Experience ✨

The recovery after my first C-section was nothing like I had imagined. The next day when I woke up from the anesthesia, I was overwhelmed by the heaviness in my body. I had always known that recovery from surgery would be challenging, but I never truly understood the depth of the struggle until I experienced it firsthand.

My body felt as if it didn't belong to me. I remember lying in that hospital bed, feeling completely drained and immobilized. My muscles were weak, and the simplest movements, like trying to sit up or shift my position, felt impossible. The weight of my body was a constant pressure, and I needed support just to stand. It wasn't just exhaustion; it was as if my entire body had been reset and was now learning how to move again.

Even the act of standing up was a monumental task. My feet felt heavy, almost as if they were cemented to the floor. It took everything I had to push myself up, and when I finally did, the effort was so intense that I felt lightheaded and dizzy. With every step, my body screamed in protest, and I had to move very slowly, carefully placing one foot in front of the other, as if walking through molasses. The sharp pain from the incision under my stomach was a constant reminder of what my body had just endured.

Thank God for the lavatory being in the room. It might seem like a small thing, but being able to use the restroom without having to leave the room was a lifesaver. Each trip felt like a mini journey, and the thought of walking to a public restroom or navigating hallways while still so vulnerable was overwhelming.

I can clearly recall the first time my relatives came to visit. I was still struggling, trying to adjust to my new reality. One of them, trying to lighten the mood, joked about how slow I was walking. At that moment, despite the discomfort, I couldn't help but chuckle.

But as I laughed, something unexpected happened... a sharp, shooting pain ripped through my abdomen. One of the staples holding my incision together literally popped off, and I felt it.

Oh my goodness, the pain was unlike anything I had ever experienced. It was a deep, agonizing throb right under my stomach, where the incision was healing. For a few seconds, I had to stand still and hold my stomach, trying to calm the pain and prevent any further damage. The pressure was so intense, and I could feel the rawness of my incision as if it were fresh again. It took several minutes for the pain to subside enough for me to even move, and in those moments, I felt completely vulnerable, trapped in a body that didn't feel like my own.

In the weeks that followed, the road to recovery remained challenging. I was constantly reminded of my limitations, of the physical and emotional strain of healing. But I also learned to be patient with myself. I had to rely on others for the simplest of things like helping me sit up, bringing me meals, and supporting me as I took those slow, painful walks. The most frustrating part was the sense of helplessness that accompanied each step. I felt like I was losing control of my own body.

But little by little, I began to see improvement. Each day, I took tiny steps toward healing, I mean literally and figuratively. I started to feel like myself again, even though it was a different version of myself. I came to appreciate the strength of my body in a way I never had before. The emotional toll was just as significant as the physical one, but in time, I grew more resilient. I learned to lean into the discomfort, to accept help, and to trust that healing takes time, even if it doesn't happen on my timetable.

The recovery process was long and difficult, but looking back, I realize how far I've come. I learned that it's okay to not be okay right away, that healing doesn't happen in a straight line, and that asking for help is not a weakness but an act of strength.

Baby Joy aka Rufredo

Chapter Two

Angel

The Second Journey

The second pregnancy was a strange mix of familiar and unfamiliar. It was as if I'd already done this before, yet every moment still felt like a new adventure. My body had been through this once, but now it was changing in unexpected ways, and my emotions were on a constant rollercoaster. With my first pregnancy, there were the usual discomforts, the blissful glow that people always talked about (even if I didn't feel very glowy), and the final anticipation of the big day. But the second time around, it was different, more intense and a little more complicated.

I had been so sure that this pregnancy would go more smoothly. After all, I had already done it once. I thought I knew what to expect. But from the moment I saw those two lines on the test again, my body seemed to have its own plans.

At first, everything was going well. The nausea, though more persistent than before, was manageable. But soon, I began to notice something that felt more unusual. My appetite, which had always been a comfort during my first pregnancy, became a source of frustration. I couldn't seem to eat certain fresh fruits without feeling nauseous or, worse, getting intense stomach cramps. It wasn't just any fruit, it was the fresh ones, the ones I had loved before, that suddenly became my nemesis. Strawberries, peaches, even simple apples, they all triggered a reaction that left me doubled over and exhausted.

I felt a sense of isolation from the foods I once enjoyed. I remember staring at a bowl of fresh cherries one evening, a fruit I had once savored in the summer heat, but now I couldn't even look at them without my stomach churning. The restriction was mentally draining like being trapped in a small, confined space, longing for the freedom of something as simple as eating a piece of fruit.

As the months passed, I grew increasingly frustrated with my body. Why couldn't I eat the foods that had always been part of my normal routine? My doctor reassured me that it was a common, though rare, issue during pregnancy, likely a shift in hormones, and that it would pass. But that didn't make it any easier.

Then, at my 36-week checkup, the news I had been half-expecting finally came. My doctor advised that, just like with my first pregnancy, a C-section might be necessary. While I had hoped things might be different this time, that maybe I'd have the vaginal birth I had dreamed of after the first C-section, my body, it seemed, was going to follow its own rhythm once again.

I wasn't terrified; not like I had been the first time. It was more of a quiet resignation. The thought of another C-section wasn't the daunting experience it had once been. I knew what to expect, the sterile smell of the operating room, the cold air, the quick movement of nurses and doctors around me. What I wasn't prepared for, though, was how much more exhausted I would feel this time around. With my first pregnancy, I had been nervous, but I was also physically stronger. This time, the combination of constant discomfort from my fruit allergies, the exhaustion from chasing a toddler around, and the emotional toll of the pregnancy wore me down in ways I hadn't imagined.

The day of the C-section arrived, and as the nurses prepped me in the cold, bright room, I could feel the weight of everything, the frustration, the physical discomfort, and, of course, the excitement. The sterile smell of the hospital and the sound of machines hum around me felt oddly comforting now. Fortunately, this time my husband was by my side. I focused on the small, calming things, the rhythmic beeping of the heart monitor, the soothing whispers of the nurses, the way the world outside seemed so far away.

As the procedure began, I closed my eyes and let myself sink into the familiarity of it all, remembering how this had felt the first time, the anticipation, the waiting, the sense of something incredible just moments away. And then, like before, I heard that first cry.

It was our baby. Our second son, finally here.

This time, the C-section felt a little less like a traumatic event and a little more like a quiet resolution. The recovery was much better, although my body was a little worn from carrying this child. But as I looked at my baby, finally in my arms, all the frustration with my body melted away. The fact that I couldn't eat strawberries or peaches anymore, that didn't matter. What mattered was that we were both safe, that the wait was over, and that I was holding my second child in my arms. A little one to love and nurture, no matter how they arrived or how I had to adapt to get them here.

In the end, this pregnancy taught me patience with my body, with the process, and with the things I couldn't control. It reminded me that, sometimes, the journey is never what you expect, and the end result is always worth it, no matter how it comes.

✨ A Better Recovery: ✨
My Second C-Section Journey

The recovery after my second C-section was a completely different experience compared to my first. While I still faced the physical challenges that come with major surgery, the healing process felt more manageable, and I was amazed at how much better I felt. The heaviness I had felt after my first surgery seemed to lift much quicker this time around, and I could tell from the start that this recovery would be less daunting.

From the very beginning, I felt an overwhelming sense of relief and joy. Unlike the first time, I didn't feel immobilized or completely drained. I was able to hold my baby right away, and that moment was one of the most beautiful of my entire journey. My baby, Jeru, latched on quickly and began breastfeeding with ease. As a firm believer in breastfeeding, I felt incredibly grateful for the opportunity to bond with him in such a natural and nourishing way. Being able to provide the best milk for him right from the start brought a sense of accomplishment and connection that I hadn't fully appreciated before.

Although my body still felt heavy and sore, the difference in how I felt physically was undeniable. The next day, I was able to get out of bed on my own, a huge improvement over my first experience. It wasn't easy, but I was determined.

The pain was still there, but it didn't paralyze me. My legs and feet didn't feel as heavy as they had before. I could actually feel the strength returning to my body, and it made all the difference in my recovery.

One of the most important things I did for my healing was getting up and moving around. I started walking the hallway independently, which helped with my blood flow and played a crucial role in speeding up my recovery. It was a slow, steady walk at first, but it felt empowering to regain control over my own movements. I could feel my body slowly adjusting, gaining strength with every step I took. Each walk made me more confident, and it was a reminder of how resilient the human body can be when given the time and care it needs to heal.

Amazingly, Jeru slept for 3 to 4 hours at a time, which was a huge blessing. His long naps allowed me to rest and recharge as well, something I had sorely missed during my first recovery. The rest was essential...not just for my physical healing but also for my mental well-being. I knew that every bit of sleep would help me regain my strength and prepare for the days ahead.

Even though this second recovery was much easier, I still took the time to be kind to myself. I knew that my body had just undergone a major surgery, and I had to listen to it. I paced myself and made sure to rest whenever I needed to, not pushing myself too hard. I knew that healing wasn't an instant process, and I had to honor that. But overall, the sense of progress was incredible.

The experience of recovering from my second C-section felt like a different chapter in my motherhood journey. I was able to enjoy the little moments with Jeru by holding him, breastfeeding, and bonding with him without the overwhelming discomfort I had felt before. While recovery was still a challenge, it was much more manageable this time, and I felt so much more equipped to handle it.

Looking back, I'm grateful for how far I've come. Each recovery is unique, and I've learned so much from both. I'm incredibly thankful for the strength of my body and the support system around me, and I'm even more thankful for the beautiful, healthy baby in my arms.

First day back home

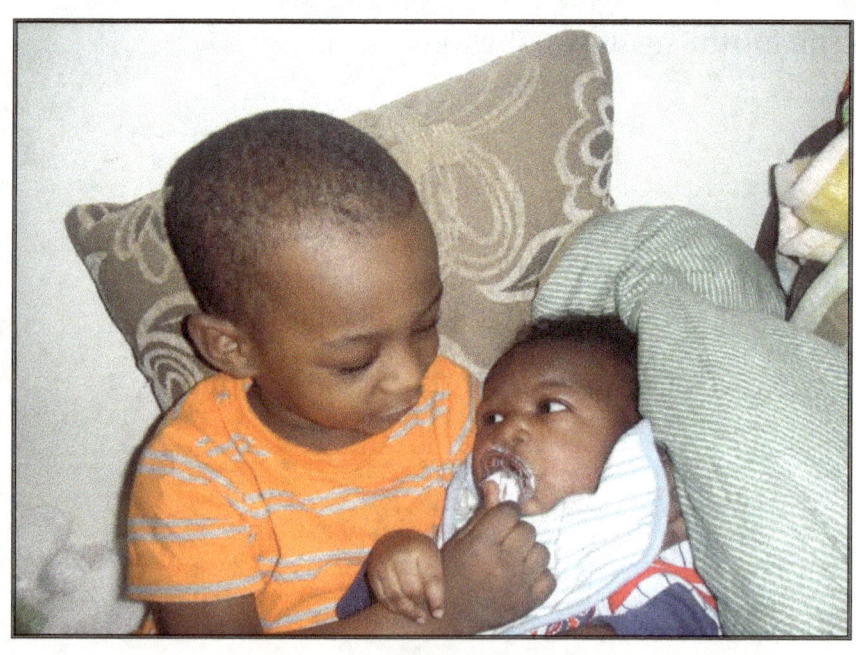

Mommy's little helper

First Professional Photo

Chapter Three

Diamond 💎

During my third pregnancy, I was filled with overwhelming joy when I found out I was having a girl. Having always dreamed of having a daughter, I had a deep longing for a little girl, but also carried a small fear that I might never have one. Growing up, I used to babysit my nieces and would always go shopping for them whenever I could. There were so many beautiful dresses and clothes for girls, and I couldn't help but imagine what it would be like to have a daughter of my own to dress up in those same adorable outfits. I prayed to God, trusting that He would grant me this wish and bless me with the child I had hoped for. When the blood results finally came back and the doctor confirmed it was a girl, I couldn't contain my excitement. I jumped up and down with sheer happiness, grateful that my prayer had been answered and my dream of having a daughter was coming true.

My sweet friend Rosa planned a beautiful baby shower
for me. She is an amazing woman, and I'm so grateful
our paths crossed in the CCC parking lot.

A Journey to Meet My Third Miracle

The decision to have a third C-section was not one I took lightly. My second pregnancy had taught me the unpredictability of labor. I'd hoped for a VBAC, but complications during labor led to an emergency C-section. This time, I wanted control. I chose a scheduled C-section to avoid the chaos and fear of another emergency. But as life would have it, plans don't always go as expected.

At the time, I was working as a kindergarten teacher. Teaching little ones is a rewarding but physically demanding job, and being in my third trimester added a new layer of challenges. My school was in a multi-story building, and my class was on the first floor. Each day, I walked my students up to the fourth-floor for their other classes and then back down after my prep period. By the end of the day, my body ached in ways I'd never experienced before.

Despite my growing belly, I had lost a significant amount of weight, leaving me skinny with a huge bump that seemed to draw curious stares everywhere I went. Every step felt heavier than the last, and my energy was dwindling. It became clear that I couldn't keep up this routine. Reluctantly, I decided to take a leave of absence earlier than planned. At the time, I felt a pang of guilt, leaving my students and colleagues, but looking back, it was the best decision I could have made.

Just a week before my scheduled C-section, my daughter had other plans. One morning, I felt a familiar yet unexpected pain, a sharp, rhythmic tightening that could only mean one thing: labor. I tried to stay calm, but deep down, I knew this wasn't going to wait until the scheduled date.

We rushed to the hospital, and just as I had feared, the situation quickly escalated into another emergency C-section. As chaotic as it felt in the moment, I was relieved to be in the hands of skilled doctors who had done this before. The procedure went smoothly, and soon, I heard her first cries, a sound that made every struggle, every ache, and every step up those stairs worth it.

Holding her in my arms for the first time, I felt a deep sense of gratitude. While the journey hadn't gone as planned, it reminded me of the resilience we find in ourselves when faced with challenges. This wasn't just the story of her birth; it was a testament to the strength and adaptability motherhood requires.

Now, as I look back, I smile knowing that sometimes, even when life doesn't go according to plan, it leads to exactly where you're meant to be, with your heart fuller than you ever thought possible.

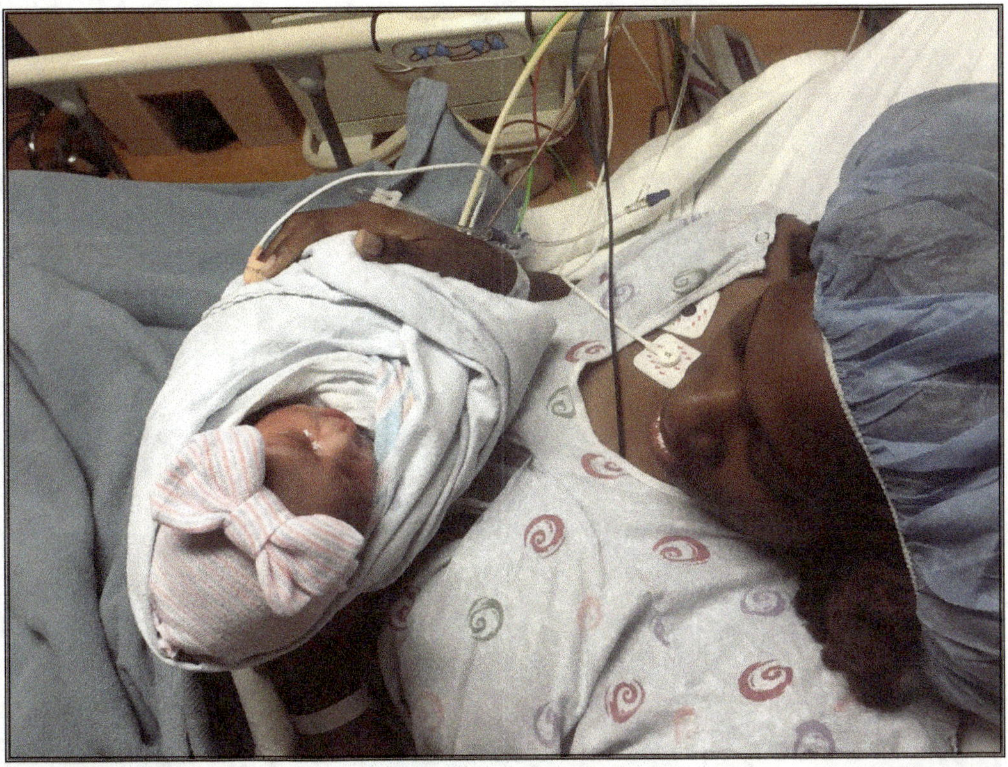

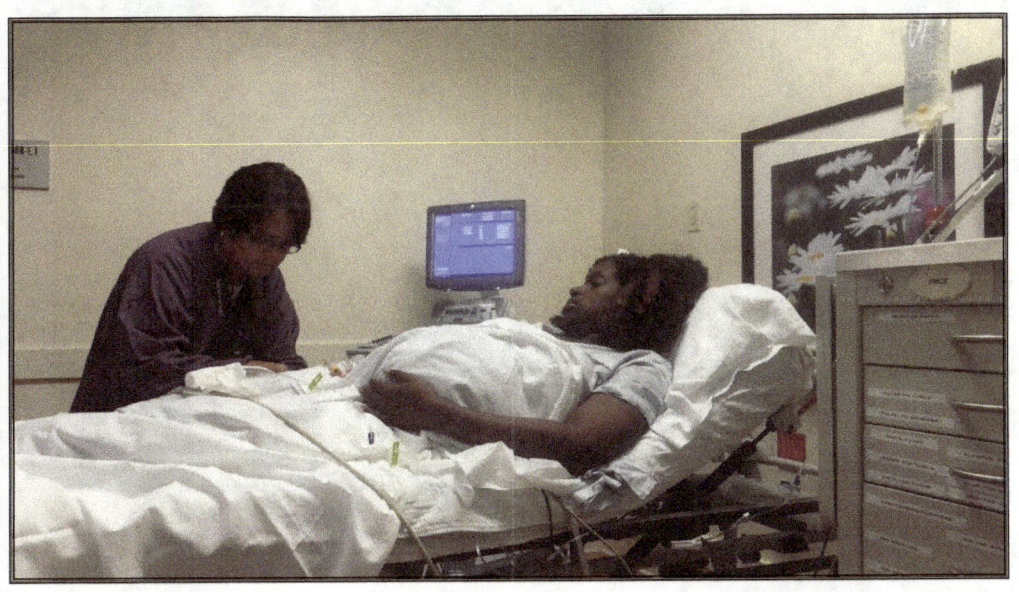

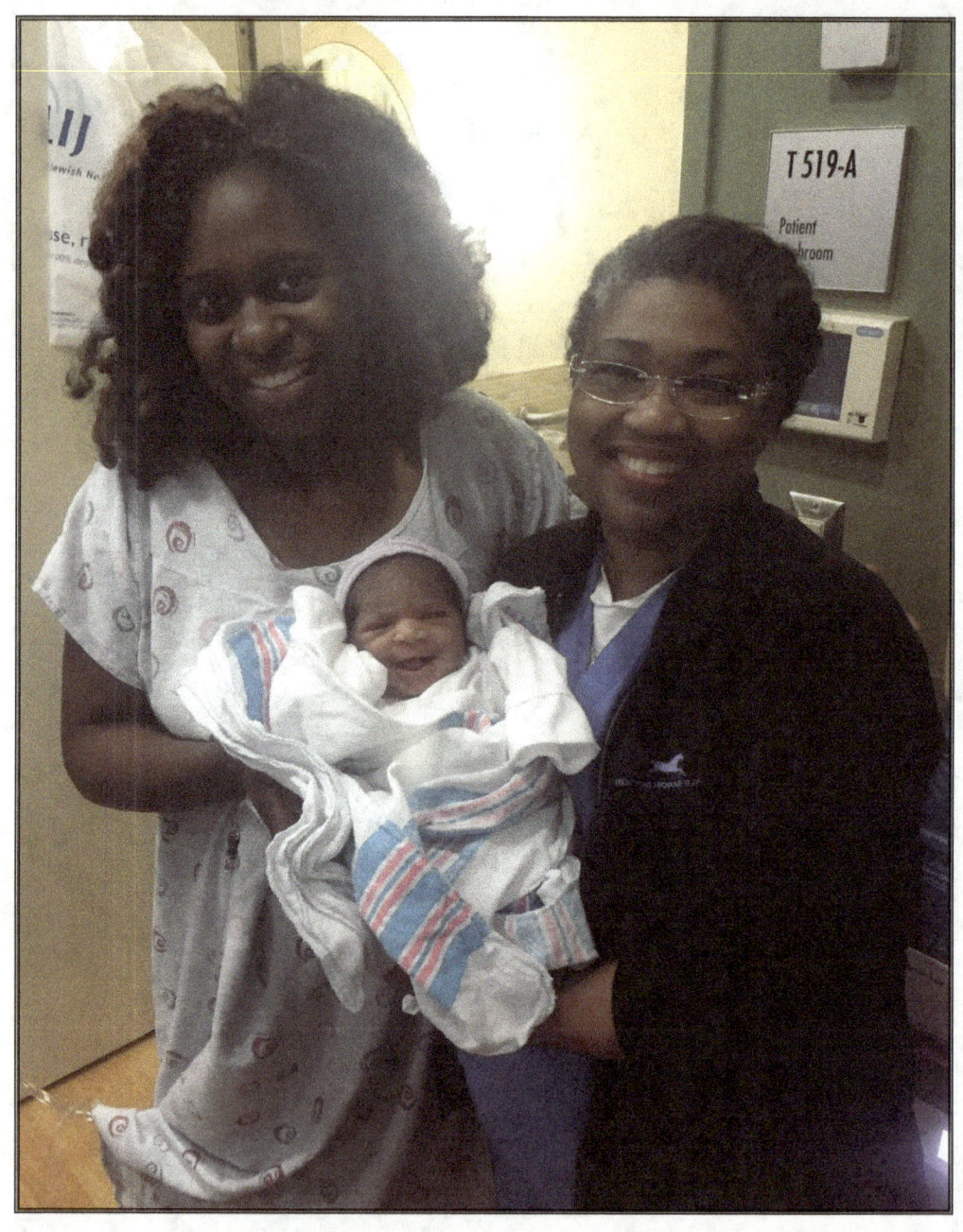

✨ Recovery Journey ✨

Every step I took was like a battle. My body felt like it had been shattered, and the idea of walking to the restroom was daunting. Thankfully, there was a lavatory in my room, but each trip felt like I was climbing a mountain in slow motion.

The physical pain was just one part of it. I felt defeated, weak, and less than myself. I had to remind myself that healing wasn't just about my body but my mind, too. I was learning that it was okay to feel vulnerable and to ask for help when I needed it.

As the days went by, the pain didn't vanish, but it became more bearable. I could finally walk to the restroom without needing support, and that felt like a small victory. My body, slow to heal, was starting to regain its strength.

In the end, I learned that recovery is not linear, nor is it just about physical healing. It's about embracing vulnerability, accepting help, and recognizing your own resilience. My body may have taken time to heal, but my heart and mind grew stronger with every day.

Chapter Four

Sweetness

The Unexpected Blessing:
Pregnancy with My Fourth Child

When I first saw the positive pregnancy test, a wave of emotions flooded over me like disbelief, excitement, and a sense of surprise. I had never imagined being pregnant again, let alone with my fourth child. It wasn't something I had planned for, and to be honest, I felt a little overwhelmed. The fact that I was about to welcome another baby, after already having three, felt surreal. I'd been through the pregnancy journey before, but this time, it was different. I had to be cautious, especially since I knew that most OB-GYNs recommend no more than three C-sections due to the risks involved. That fact was always in the back of my mind as I processed the news. I knew this would be a delicate journey, but as the days went by, I couldn't help but feel a growing sense of excitement.

My family had concerns about my fourth pregnancy, particularly because they knew the risks were higher with each successive cesarean. In my case, I had been labeled as a high-risk pregnancy because of my previous preeclampsia diagnosis. This raised extra caution not only for my medical team but also for my loved ones, who were understandably anxious about the road ahead.

With this in mind, I took every precaution during my pregnancy. I closely monitored what I ate, made sure to stay as active as I could, and paid attention to every detail of my physical well-being. I knew this would be a delicate journey, but as the days went by, I couldn't help but feel a growing sense of excitement.

As time passed, I started to open my heart to the idea of this unexpected blessing. I realized that the love and joy a new baby brings could never be planned or predicted, it just happens. So, despite my initial hesitation, I embraced the pregnancy, hoping that this time I would be able to carry it full-term and deliver on the scheduled date, avoiding an emergency C-section. I made it my mission to take extra precautions to ensure this would be the case. I was careful with my diet, listened to my body, and made sure to keep all my doctor's appointments. I wanted to ensure a smooth and planned delivery, for both my health and the baby's.

Around 7-8 weeks into the pregnancy, I stumbled across a product called Intelligender, which claimed to predict the sex of your baby early on. Of course, I knew it wasn't scientifically proven, but the fun of having a little early sneak peek into the baby's gender was too tempting to resist. I was filled with anticipation as I waited for the results, part of me hoping for another girl. It was all in good fun, a way to feel more connected to the baby growing inside me before the official ultrasound. The result? It was a girl! Of course, I would find out much later that the result was correct.

Physically, I felt amazing throughout the pregnancy. I was energized, my body was cooperating, and I didn't have the usual aches and pains that sometimes come with carrying a baby. I had this sense of vitality and strength that was encouraging. I knew it might not last, but I was grateful for it while it did. Around 24 weeks, I had my second son join me for an ultrasound appointment. I had been keeping the news of the pregnancy fairly quiet at home, but now it was time to share the big news with him.

When I told him, he was absolutely shocked. "Another sibling?" he asked, his eyes wide with disbelief. At first, he didn't believe me, thinking I was joking. He's used to being the center of attention, and the idea of sharing it with another sibling didn't sit well with him. I could see the confusion and fear in his eyes. He didn't understand how his life was about to change. His first instinct was that the love and attention I had always showered on him would somehow diminish when the new baby arrived. He was worried that the arrival of a new sibling would mean less of me for him.

The concern was real, and it broke my heart to see him feel that way. I tried to reassure him, explaining that love doesn't divide and it multiplies. I told him that he would always be my baby, no matter how many siblings he had. But as much as I tried to comfort him, I knew that he would need time to process this new chapter in our family.

In the weeks that followed, I watched my second son slowly warm to the idea of becoming an older brother. It wasn't an instant shift, but with every ultrasound, every little kick, and every baby name suggestion, he began to soften. Meanwhile, my oldest son and daughter were absolutely thrilled to learn they were getting a little sister. Their excitement was contagious, making the whole experience even more meaningful. Over time, my second son also grew excited about the idea of having a sibling, though it wasn't without its moments of anxiety and adjustment along the way.

The pregnancy, like any, was a journey filled with highs and lows, but I could already sense the changes it was bringing to our family. This little life was going to be a huge blessing, and while the road to delivery would come with its challenges, I couldn't wait to meet the baby I was carrying.

Pregnant with my fourth child

For much of the pregnancy, I felt great and was optimistic about how things were going. However, in the final trimester, the physical toll of carrying a larger baby started to become more noticeable, as I felt more tired and uncomfortable.

Around 31–32 weeks, just like with my previous pregnancies, my healthcare provider scheduled a repeat cesarean, set to take place about two weeks before my due date. The surgery would be performed at a hospital in Queens where I had delivered my two previous children via C-section. I had always had a positive experience at that hospital, which brought me some peace of mind as the date approached.

Before the surgery, I had to go in for a preoperative assessment, a standard procedure that ensured everything was in order for the upcoming procedure. It was another step in the process, it was a reminder that I was about to face yet another significant moment in my journey toward motherhood.

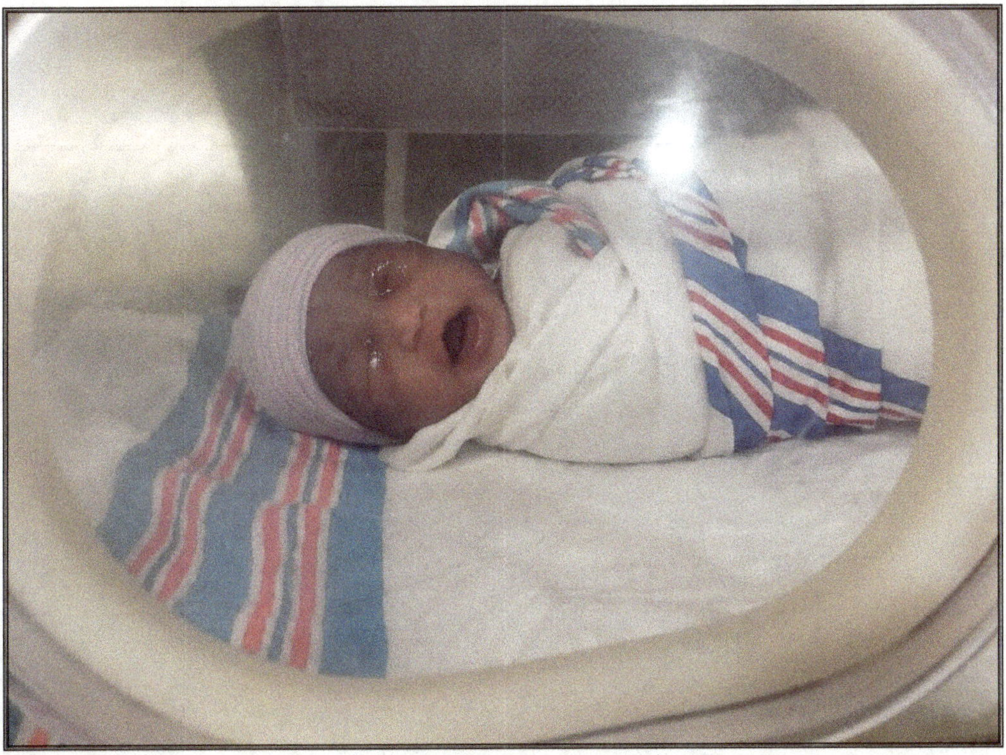

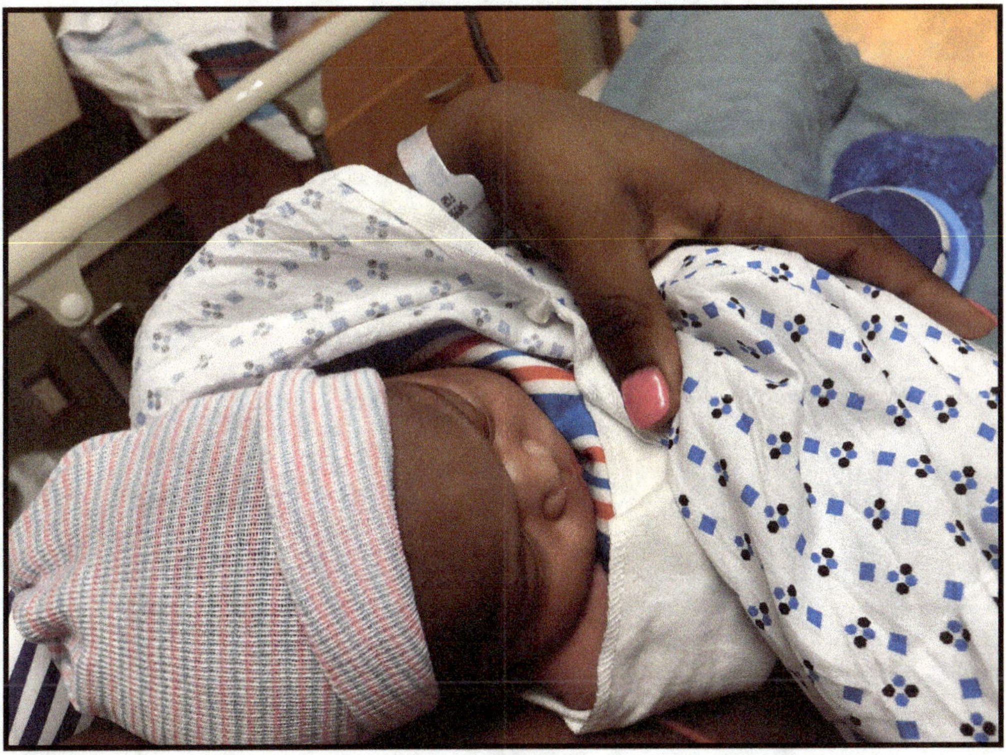

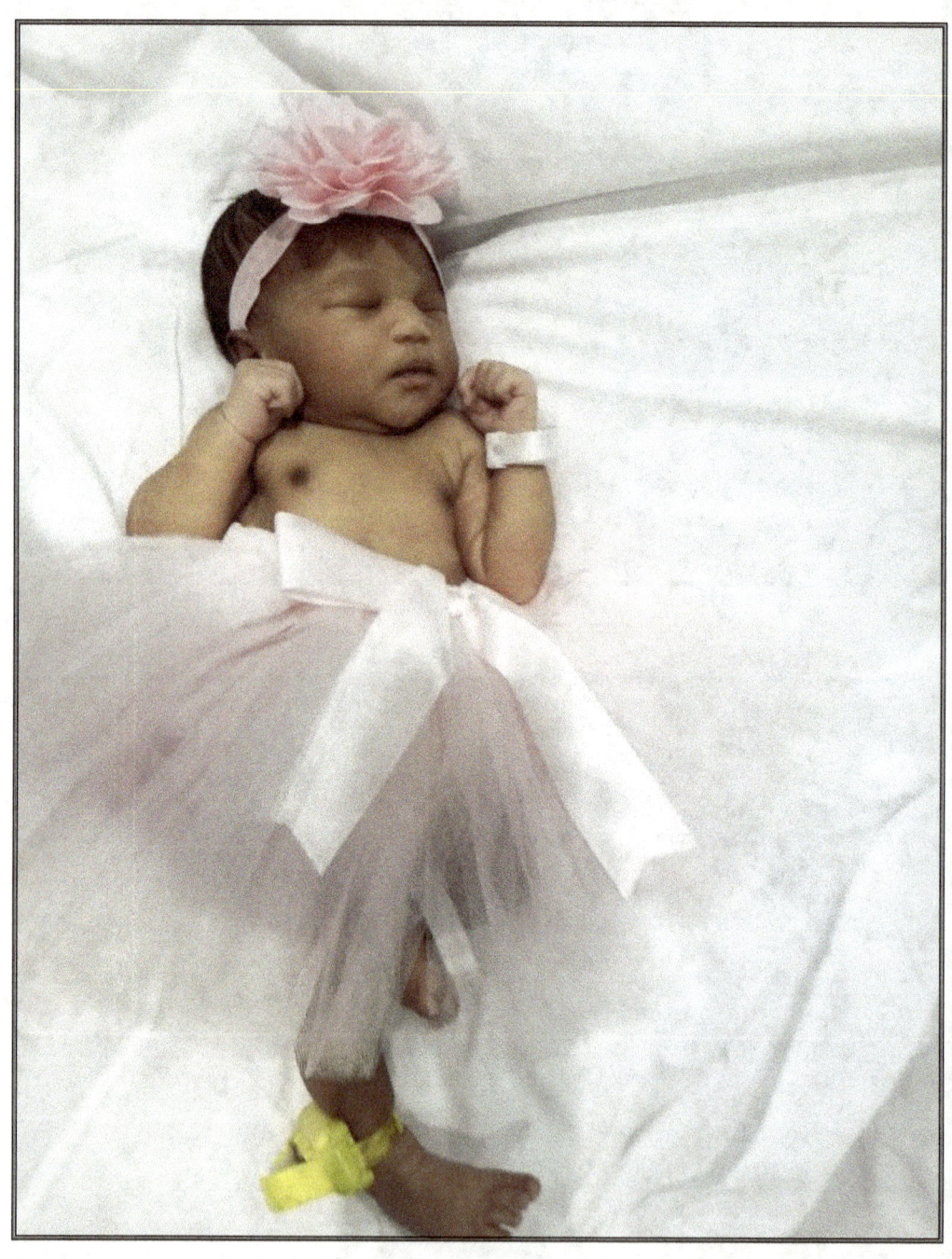

✨Recovery✨

After my fourth c-section, I was pleasantly surprised by how well I was recovering. The next day, I was able to walk independently, a feat I hadn't expected so soon. As I regained my strength, my family came to visit, filling the room with love and joy. The hospital photoshoot with my sons and daughters was a beautiful moment I will cherish forever. The photographers captured the joy and love we shared in that sacred space, freezing time in images that would become lifelong treasures. As I gazed at my newborn girl, swaddled in a soft blanket, I felt a deep sense of awe. She was so tiny, yet so perfect in every way. My three-year-old daughter sat, her eyes wide with wonder as she took in her new sister, and I couldn't help but smile at the thought that I had just been blessed with two daughters.

I had always dreamt of having a family that felt complete, but it was only in that moment, holding my two girls and watching my sons interact with them, that I truly realized how much my heart had expanded. There, in that hospital room, surrounded by the people I loved most, I felt like the family I had long envisioned was finally whole. For the first time, I understood the feeling of completeness, and it was more beautiful and fulfilling than I could have ever imagined.

My second princess

My two daughters

Chapter Five

Treasure

My Fifth C-Section Experience

When my husband expressed his desire for another child, I felt a mix of emotions. I was open to the idea, especially because my gynecologist had reassured me that I had healed well from my previous cesareans. However, she also cautioned me about the increased risks of having multiple C-sections and advised that this would likely be my last pregnancy. It would be my fifth C-section, and the risks associated with it were something I needed to consider carefully.

Despite the warnings, my pregnancy went smoothly. I didn't experience the usual morning sickness that so many others talk about, but I did find that I couldn't tolerate certain fruits and salads, something I hadn't experienced in my prior pregnancies. It was a bit strange, but I adjusted as best as I could.

This time around, the challenge was not just the pregnancy itself, but the added responsibility of raising my four other children while caring for myself and the baby growing inside me. Balancing it all was tough, juggling school runs, housework, and being present for my older kids while also managing the physical and emotional demands of carrying a baby for the fifth time was a delicate act.

Even though I was tired and occasionally overwhelmed, I knew that I had to keep pushing forward for the sake of my family and the new life we were about to welcome. There were moments of doubt, but there was also a lot of love and anticipation as we prepared for the arrival of our little one. Despite the challenges, I was ready to give it my all one more time and embrace the joys (and the exhaustion) that would come with having another child.

The experience was a testament to the strength and resilience of mothers. While the risks were real and the challenges were many, the love for my family and the excitement of welcoming another blessing into our lives kept me moving forward.

Rullen smells so good.

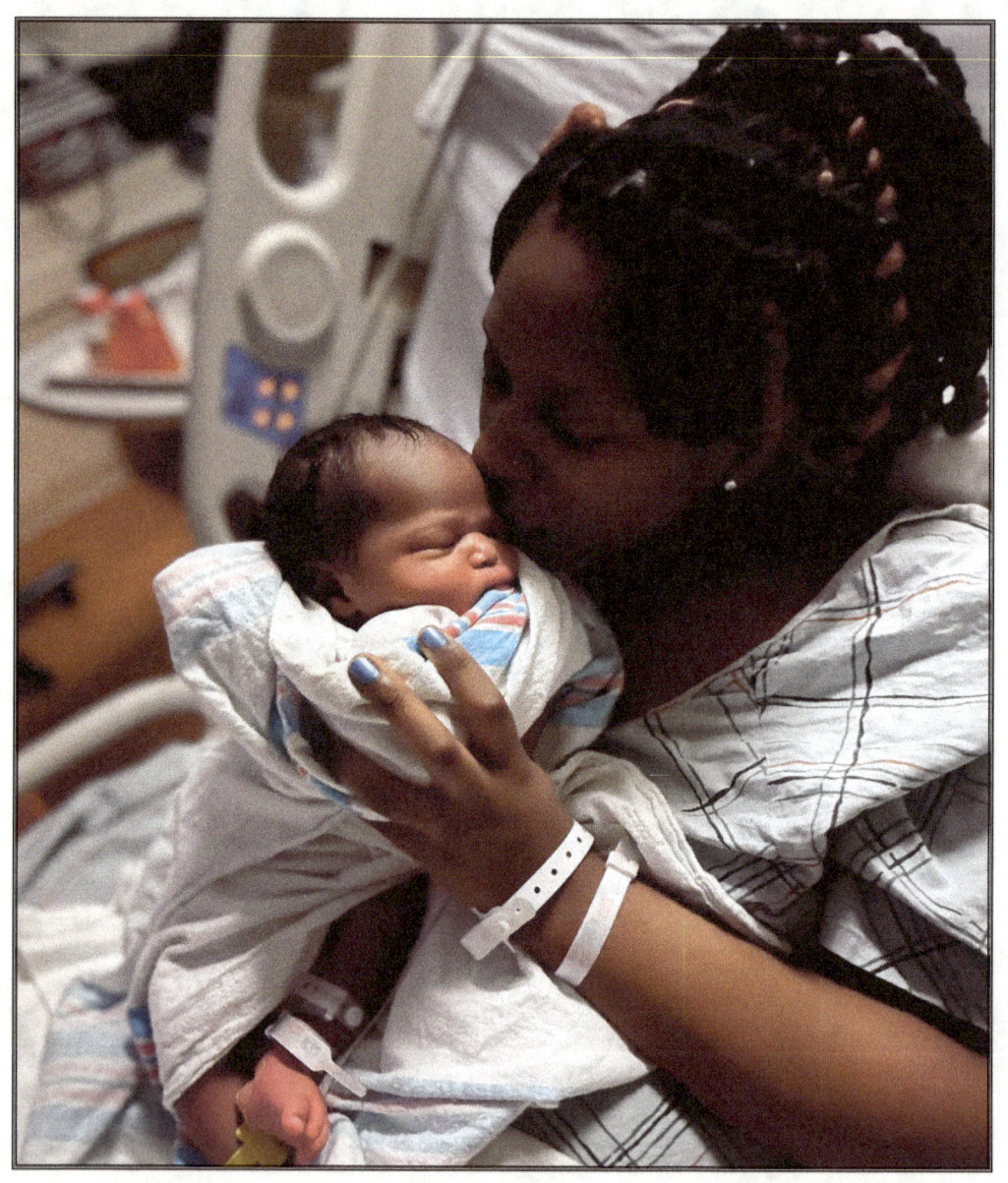

First Kiss

Post Delivery

Initial bonding time is essential; skin to skin and breastfeeding are meaningful.

✨Recovery✨

After my fifth C-section, I initially felt good, and my OB-GYN applied tape to my incision. However, a few days later, after the tape was removed, I noticed that the incision had opened slightly on the right side. This was a new experience for me, as it had never happened with my previous C-sections, and I became quite worried. Concerned about the healing process, I quickly scheduled an appointment with my GYN.

When I saw my doctor, they reassured me that the incision still looked good overall and suggested I place a pad to catch any discharge from the wound. I also used band-aids for added protection. In addition, I was advised to reduce my movement and take extra care to rest, which led me to stay on the first floor of my house. Climbing the stairs to my bedroom was too difficult, so I set up a temporary resting space downstairs to avoid straining myself.

During this time, I focused on slowing down, taking things one step at a time, and trusting in the healing process. I prayed for strength, asking God to help me stay calm and to guide me through this challenging moment. Despite the setback, I continued to rely on my faith and took comfort in knowing that with patience, rest, and trust, my body would heal.

Tapes on the incision

Opening on the incision

Chapter Six

Risk of having Cesarean

Healthcare Provider/Team may recommend having a C-Section due to:

- Baby in an unusual position

- Twins or more

- A problem with the placenta

- Previous c-section (may suggest a repeat c-section)

Risk of having a Cesarean

Mother	Baby
Blood Loss	Breathing Issues
Infection	Surgical Injury
Blood Clots	
High Blood Pressure	

For a Scheduled Cesarean:

You will be advised to schedule a procedure typically called a "preoperative assessment". This is a routine check-up that occurs a few days before a scheduled C-section. The healthcare provider ensures that both you and your baby are ready for surgery. The assessment may involve:

1. **Medical History Review:** Your doctor will review your medical history, previous pregnancies, and any health issues.

2. **Physical Examination:** This could include monitoring your blood pressure, checking for swelling, and listening to the baby's heartbeat.

3. **Blood Tests:** You may have blood drawn to check your hemoglobin levels, and blood type.

4. **Ultrasound:** Sometimes, a final ultrasound may be done to check the baby's position, size, and placental location.

5. **Discussion of the Procedure:** Your doctor will explain the C-section procedure, anesthesia options, potential risks, and the expected recovery process.

6. **Instructions for the Day of Surgery:** You'll receive specific instructions about when to stop eating or drinking, medications you may need to take, and what to bring to the hospital.

Chapter Seven

Vaginal Birth After Cesarean

Do you know what a VBAC is?

Don't worry, most people don't. I didn't either, not until after I had my first C-section. I was terrified at the thought of having more children because I didn't want to go through that kind of pain again.

One day, while at an African braiding salon in Brooklyn, I ran into a family friend from church. We chatted and caught up on life. During our conversation, she mentioned that she also had a C-section with her first child. But for her second, she had something I had never heard of before, a VBAC, which stands for Vaginal Birth After Cesarean.

That moment changed everything for me. I went home and began researching VBACs. I learned that while some OB-GYNs support it, others view it as risky and don't recommend it. Fortunately, another friend from church told me about her supportive OB-GYN based in Queens, NY and that gave me hope.

Chapter Eight

Interviews

Interview- Nefertiti Wade

Nefertiti Wade's C-Section Experience:
A Journey of Strength and Resilience

Nefertiti Wade had a relatively smooth pregnancy, carrying her baby to full term and experiencing a positive labor and delivery. However, her recovery after the C-section was a different story. Before her delivery, she had been very swollen—a condition that persisted postpartum. Nefertiti is a petite woman, and the swelling did not subside after the birth. Along with the swelling, she experienced fatigue.

Although the doctors recommended a blood transfusion, Nefertiti asked if she could try to boost her blood count naturally. They gave her the green light to try. Due to her lack of understanding about what a healthy blood level should be, she opted not to get the transfusion. Discharged with a low blood count and continued swelling, she went home, but something didn't feel right.

That night, Nefertiti felt strange in her chest and called the doctor. They suggested she take Percocet, a painkiller, but she knew that wouldn't address her symptoms. She wasn't in pain, but she felt uneasy. She stayed awake all night, continuing to feel off, and called her doctor's office the next morning. The nurse immediately instructed her to go to the hospital.

Once at the hospital, tests revealed that Nefertiti had developed preeclampsia, a condition marked by persistent high blood pressure during pregnancy or the postpartum period. It is often accompanied by high levels of protein in the urine and can involve complications like decreased blood platelets, kidney or liver trouble, fluid in the lungs, and even seizures or visual disturbances.

After being diagnosed, Nefertiti required a blood transfusion and the removal of excess fluid from her body. If she had taken the Percocet, it's possible her condition would have worsened, and she may not be here today.

Nefertiti's experience highlights the crucial importance of self-advocacy during recovery. Her quick response to her symptoms ensured that she received the care she desperately needed. Despite the challenges she faced after the procedure, Nefertiti's story is a powerful reminder of the strength required to navigate the complexities of both the joys and struggles of motherhood.

Nefertiti Wade

Interviewee: Shayla Patrick

Shayla Patrick's C-Section Journey:
From Struggle to Empowerment

Shayla Patrick's journey through childbirth has been shaped by both difficult and empowering experiences. Having undergone three C-sections, her first experience left an indelible mark on her. During her first delivery, Shayla faced significant challenges—not just physically, but emotionally. She felt that one of the nurses denied her medication, a moment she believes may have been influenced by racial bias. As a Black mother, Shayla couldn't shake the feeling that her pain was dismissed, leaving her feeling powerless and unheard during one of the most vulnerable times in her life.

However, Shayla's second C-section experience was a stark contrast. After the challenges of her first birth, she was determined to approach her second delivery with a sense of empowerment and control. This time, her medical team was more attentive, and the care she received was supportive and respectful. Shayla felt listened to, and the experience left her feeling more confident and at ease.

Despite the difficulties of her first experience, Shayla's journey through her C-sections has been one of growth and resilience. Her story highlights not only the importance of quality care and respect in the birthing process but also the need for advocacy and self-empowerment, especially for Black mothers who may face discrimination in the healthcare system.

Shayla's experiences serve as a reminder that every mother deserves to be treated with dignity, compassion, and respect during childbirth. Her story is a testament to the strength it takes to overcome adversity, and to find healing and confidence in the face of a challenging journey.

Shayla Patrick

Interviewee: Gloria Louissaint

Gloria Louissaint's journey through multiple C-sections has been filled with challenges, but it has also shown her the importance of self-advocacy and finding a medical team that respects her needs. With each experience, she learned more about what it takes to navigate a difficult but ultimately rewarding process.

First C-Section

Gloria Louissaint's first pregnancy was challenging, and her experience with the C-section was far from ideal. At just a young age, she felt discriminated against by the medical team, who seemed to underestimate her ability to handle the situation. Her labor began at 9 a.m. and stretched all the way until 9 p.m., making the long hours even more grueling.

By the time the medical team informed her that she had developed a fever and the chills, they explained that an infection was likely the cause. The team insisted on a C-section, citing their concern for the infection's impact on the baby. Initially, Gloria hesitated, but after about two hours of labor, the pain became overwhelming. She decided to opt for an epidural, though she was terrified. The thought of moving and possibly being paralyzed from the waist down was a huge fear for her.

The recovery was painful and challenging. She had staples placed along her incision, which were removed before she left the hospital. However, she didn't get to see her baby until three days later, which added to her emotional distress. She spent a total of four days in the hospital, while her baby had to stay for an additional three days, monitored for issues.

Second C-Section

Her second C-section was a much more positive experience. The medical team was more compassionate and respectful, addressing her concerns in a way that made her feel heard. This time, she was informed that her contractions posed a risk of rupturing the prior incision, which led her to agree to a repeat C-section.

For this procedure, she was given a spinal block, numbing her from the waist down. The recovery process was smoother this time. She felt more alert and active sooner, which gave her a sense of relief.

She was able to see her baby immediately after the birth, and the baby stayed in the room with her during her four-day hospital stay.

Third C-Section

Gloria's third pregnancy was a smoother and more positive experience overall. It was a girl, and the pregnancy itself went well. However, she made the decision to switch doctors just before the procedure. Her previous OB-GYN was planning to use staples for the incision, but she decided to change doctors to one who used tape instead. The decision was motivated by her desire to have a more comfortable experience and better care.

Once again, she received a spinal block for pain relief. However, she did feel pressure during the surgery due to excessive tissue buildup in the area of the incision. The new OB-GYN was thorough and removed the extra tissue, which alleviated the discomfort. Despite the procedure going well, the incision site remained very sensitive for quite some time.

Fourth C-Section

For her fourth pregnancy, Gloria found out she was expecting around the three-month mark. Her pregnancy required some additional medical attention, as she had to undergo a blood infusion at nine months due to low iron and low blood count.

Despite these challenges, Gloria had a relatively good recovery. She received a spinal block for pain management and, after the procedure, was alert and able to stand and walk around a bit sooner than in previous surgeries. She was also able to hold her baby right away, enjoying skin-to-skin contact.

She stayed in the hospital for four days, during which she received an iron infusion via IV. Her baby, however, had to stay an additional three days for monitoring. The baby had been born with meconium aspiration syndrome, which meant they had to keep an eye on his ability to breathe. Gloria was emotional during this time, struggling to leave him behind. The hospital monitored him closely, ensuring he was able to breathe on his own, which he successfully did by the second day.

Advice for Future Birth Plans

Having gone through multiple C-sections, Gloria has some valuable advice for others preparing for childbirth. First and foremost, she emphasizes the importance of asking questions, lots of them. It's essential to understand why you are being advised to have a C-section and to feel that you have options. In her experience, medical teams can sometimes make it feel like you have no choice, but it's important to advocate for yourself. She suggests looking into private OB-GYN practices where doctors are more accessible and willing to answer questions. Having someone from their team who is dedicated to supporting you and addressing your concerns can make a huge difference in your overall experience.

Gloria Louissaint

Pregnant with baby # 4

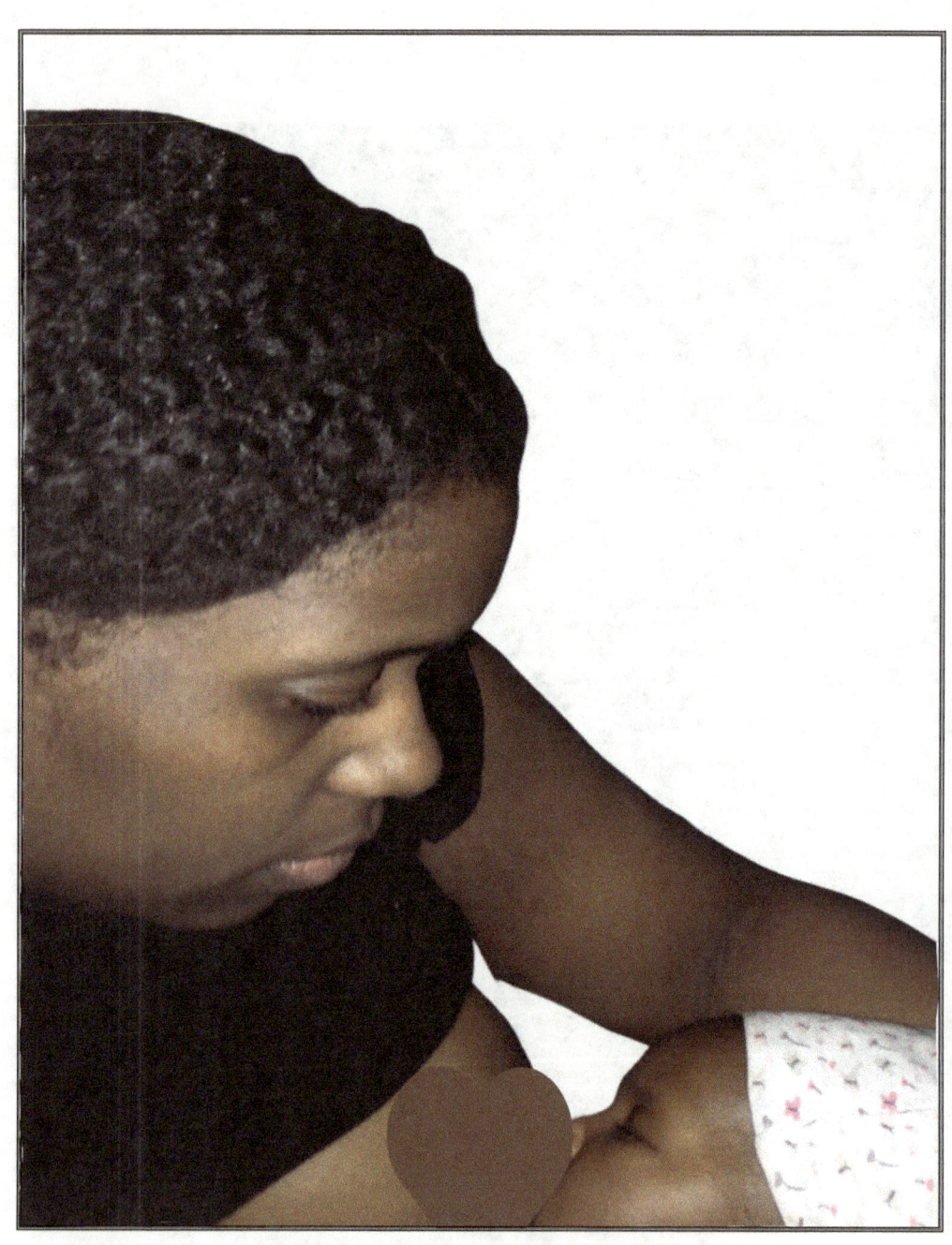

Breast milk is the best milk

Today, this resilient mother is available
to help you tell your story.

Book Coach Ruth

Poems

Pregnant Mom

A mother's love is incomparable,

An unexplainable inner touch.

The pounding heart, growing each day in the womb,

A spectacular feeling,

A love a mother will fight for, if ever threatened.

Baby # 5

Postpartum Mom

Wow, the baby is here!

Congratulations!

Mixed emotions flood your heart and mind,

A bundle of joy to protect and guide in this world.

A blessing to cherish and nurture.

You've got this!

Enjoy your precious pearl.

Happy Mothering!

Create positive memories

Child Rearing Mom

Look at your blessing,

Growing so fast right before your eyes.

Your precious pearl is letting go of your hand to explore life.

Continue to lead, model, and observe,

For your pearl is watching and taking mental notes.

Seek support when needed, Stay positive,

And remember to relax, rest, and make time for self-care.

Happy Mothering!

At my favorite place with my babies

Preparing for a C-Section

1. **Understand the Procedure:** Familiarize yourself with what will happen during a C-section. Knowing the steps involved can help ease your anxiety and make you feel more in control.

2. **Talk to Your Doctor:** Have a detailed discussion with your doctor about the reasons for the C-section, what to expect, and any concerns you may have. Ask about the anesthesia, recovery process, and potential risks.

3. **Create a Birth Plan:** Even though you may be having a C-section, you can still have preferences, such as having your partner with you in the operating room, playing calming music, or delayed cord clamping (if safe and feasible).

4. **Prepare for Hospital Stay:** Pack your hospital bag with essentials, including:

    -   Loose, comfortable clothing
    -   Personal hygiene items
    -   Maternity pads and comfy underwear
    -   Phone and charger
    -   A blanket or pillow from home for extra comfort

5. **Arrange Postpartum Help:** Since recovery from a C-section can take time, arrange for help at home after you leave the hospital. Ask for support with meal prep, cleaning, and baby care.

6. Plan for Mobility: Post-surgery, you'll be moving slowly, so set up your living space for ease. Consider things like having everything you need within arm's reach (water, snacks, baby supplies) and arranging a comfortable spot for feeding.

7. **Practice Relaxation:** Use relaxation techniques like deep breathing or guided meditation in the weeks leading up to your C-section. These can help calm your nerves and reduce stress.

8. **Avoid Eating or Drinking Before Surgery:** You'll typically be asked not to eat or drink for a certain period before the surgery. Follow your doctor's guidelines to ensure the procedure goes smoothly.

9. **Understand the Anesthesia Options:** Discuss with your healthcare provider what type of anesthesia will be used (epidural or spinal block) and how it will affect you. You may be awake but numbed from the waist down.

10. **Plan for Your Baby's Care:** If possible, discuss how your baby will be cared for immediately after birth. Depending on the hospital, your baby might be placed on your chest for skin-to-skin contact or handed to your partner.

11. **Prepare for Recovery:** Recovery from a C-section typically takes longer than vaginal delivery. Mentally

prepare for a slower recovery process. Focus on taking it easy, getting rest, and following your doctor's advice for incision care and activity restrictions.

12. **Stay Open to Changes:** While you may have planned for a vaginal birth, it's important to be flexible in case circumstances require a C-section. Embrace the process, knowing it's a safe option for both you and your baby.

13. **Have a Support System:** Make sure you have emotional and physical support from your partner, family, or friends both before and after the surgery.

14. **Ask About Breastfeeding After C-Section:** If you plan to breastfeed, talk to your medical team about strategies for breastfeeding after a C-section. You may need to experiment with different positions to find what feels most comfortable.

15. **Consider Your Mental Health:** After a C-section, you might have mixed emotions. It's normal to feel disappointed if you didn't have the birth you envisioned. Reach out for support if you're struggling emotionally.

PREGNANCY
Weight Tracker

Week 2		Week 15		Week 28	
Week 3		Week 16		Week 29	
Week 4		Week 17		**Week 30**	
Week 5		Week 18		Week 31	
Week 6		Week 19		Week 32	
Week 7		**Week 20**		Week 33	
Week 8		Week 21		Week 34	
Week 9		Week 22		Week 35	
Week 10		Week 23		Week 36	
Week 11		Week 24		Week 37	
Week 12		Week 25		Week 38	
Week 13		Week 26		Week 39	
Week 14		Week 27		**Week 40**	

SAMPLE
BIRTH PLAN FOR

_____

LABOR PREFERENCES

Environment

_____ Dim lighting
_____ Soft music
_____ Limited visitors

Pain Relief

_____ Epidural
_____ Natural methods (breathing
exercises, massage)
_____ Other medications

Hydration and Nutrition

_____ IV fluids if necessary
_____ Snacking as allowed

Monitoring Baby

_____ Continuous fetal monitoring
_____ Intermittent monitoring

Movement During Labor

_____ Freedom to walk
_____ Use of birthing ball or chair

Induction if Needed

Yes/No | Preferences of method

_____
_____
_____
_____

DELIVERY PREFERENCES

Rooming-In with Baby

Yes/No

Baby's First Bath

_____ In-room
_____ Nurse-assisted

Feeding

_____ Breastfeeding
_____ Bottle feeding
_____ Combination

Visitors

Yes/No | Visitors list

_____
_____
_____
_____
_____

EMERGENCY CONTACTS

_____
_____
_____
_____
_____

Pregnancy *milestones*

MILESTONE	DATE
Pregnancy Test	
First Prenatal Visit	
Announcing the Pregnancy	
First Ultrasound	
Finding Out the Baby's Sex	
Feeling the First Movements	
Second Trimester Ultrasound	
Choosing the Baby's Name	
Baby Shower	
Prenatal Classes	
Maternity Photoshoot	
First Kick Felt by Partner	
Creating a Birth Plan	
Packing the Hospital Bag	
Last Pre-Baby Vacation	

Acknowledgements

I want to take a moment to honor my own strength and resilience, as it has been a constant source of power throughout my journey. Every scar I carry tells a story of survival, growth, and transformation. These scars are not just marks of pain but symbols of the battles I've faced and reminders of how far I've come and the strength I've discovered within myself.

Through every challenge, I have learned to stand tall, to rise again after falling, and to embrace my scars as part of my unique story. I am proud of who I've become, and I recognize the courage it has taken to keep moving forward despite the obstacles life has presented.

This book is a testament to that strength, and I dedicate it to anyone who has ever felt broken, lost, or unsure. May you know that you, too, are capable of finding the power within to heal, to grow, and to thrive.

To mommy,

I am here today because of my cheerleader. I want to express my endless thanks to my incredible mother, whose love and support have been my constant source of strength throughout my life. From the time I was a young girl, she has been my biggest cheerleader, encouraging me to reach for the stars and reminding me of my own inner resilience.

As a young girl, I dreamt of having four children just like my mother did. However, after the difficult experience of my first c-section, I questioned that dream. Yet, it was my mother who reminded me of the importance of perseverance and the beauty of unconditional love.

Thank you, Mom, for showing up when I needed you most, like coming to the hospital, cooking for me, and caring for me as I recovered. Your nurturing spirit never wavered. Even though I couldn't fully embrace the Haitian tradition of bathing with herbs due to my surgery, your love and care filled the space with healing, and for that, I am forever grateful.

Love your baby daughter,
Ruth Lamour Fleury

To my hearts,

I am a better person due to my children. I want to express my deepest gratitude to my five beautiful children, who have shown me nothing but unconditional love and support throughout this writing journey. Their presence in my life has been a constant reminder of what truly matters, and they have always been by my side whenever I needed them.

I am incredibly honored to be their mother, and it is with love and pride that I continue to guide them through this journey called life. They inspire me every day, and their belief in me has been a source of strength I can never fully express.

To my children:

I love you all, and I thank you from the bottom of my heart. Your love has fueled this book, and I am forever grateful for each of you.

Love mommy always 🧡

To papi,

I want to express my heartfelt gratitude to my father, whose support has been a constant in my life since I was a young girl. He was always there—driving me to school, taking me to doctor visits, and showing up for parent-teacher conferences. Though we didn't always see eye to eye and sometimes bumped heads due to his old-fashioned ways, I am deeply thankful for his unwavering presence in both my childhood and adulthood.

Not only is he a dedicated father, but he is also a wonderful grandfather. His love and support for my children are evident, and they adore him.

Thank you, Dad, for being there when I needed you most—driving me to the hospital and preparing meals for me and my family as I recovered. Your care, love, and dedication have meant more than words can express.

Love,
Ruth

To Fredo,

From day one, you have been by my side. Together, we walked into parenthood with uncertainty, not always knowing what the next step would be, but we figured it out as we went. We argued, we disagreed, but through it all, we grew—learning to balance our differences and find common ground for the sake of our children.

I am truly grateful for you and for the way you show up for our family. Our children love you dearly, and I know they feel your unwavering support and presence in their lives. Thank you for being there for them and for me, through all the highs and lows.

Love,
Ruth

To my Godfather,

I am grateful for the balance in my childhood. I want to express my sincere appreciation to my incredible brother, who has always been like a second father to me. As my godfather, he has filled my life with love and nurturing, showing me affection and support that helped fill any void I felt. His belief in me, his trust in me, and the way he confides in me has always made me feel validated and deeply loved.

Thank you, my amazing brother, for being there for me through thick and thin. I'm so proud of everything you're accomplishing now, and it brings me immense joy to know that I've been able to inspire you as you move forward in your own writing journey.

Thank you for being such a loving and constant presence in my life. I am blessed to call you my brother, and I'm honored to have you by my side.

Love,
Ruth

To Nefertiti, Shayla and Gloria,

I want to take this moment to express my deepest gratitude to the three incredible moms who generously volunteered their time and shared their C-section experiences with me. Your openness and willingness to be vulnerable have taught me so much, and I am truly grateful for the wisdom you've shared.

Through our conversations, we have formed a sisterhood built on mutual support, understanding, and shared experiences. We continue to learn from each other, and together, we strive to be a source of strength for other moms in our community.

Thank you for being a part of this journey and for the bond we've created. Your support means more than words can express.

Love,
Ruth 🧡

About the Author

Ruth Fleury is an educator, author, publisher, and advocate for children's literacy and representation. In 2021, Ruth ventured into publishing with the release of her first children's book, *HYPER KID, SO THEY SAY!*, which tells the story of a boy named Rio who is misunderstood at school but finds support through an empathetic teacher . She has since authored additional works, including *Moving Rio Coloring Book, Self-Love with Positivity: The ABC of Self-Reflection Journal*, and *Soup Joumou Freedom Celebration*. Her upcoming book, Embracing Me!, is set to be released in summer 2025.

Ruth's commitment to literacy and education extends beyond her own writing. She launched a Book Coaching Program in January 2023 to assist aspiring authors in writing and publishing their books. Her work has been recognized with awards such as the Golden Wizard Book Prize and an international book award for *Soup Joumou Freedom Celebration.*

In addition to her professional achievements, Ruth is a mother of five children, two of whom have also published books through Scholars Of Tomorrow Publishing . She continues to inspire others through her dedication to storytelling, education, and community engagement.

Author's Note

Cesarean Awareness Month is essential. When I was pregnant with my first child, I had no idea what it was. I only found out the day of my labor and delivery, when I unexpectedly needed an emergency

C-section. Today, I aim to educate women who plan to get pregnant, new mothers, and first-time C-section candidates. Pregnancy and motherhood are beautiful and unique journeys for everyone.

-Ruth Fleury, M.S. Ed

www.ingramcontent.com/pod-product-compliance
Lightning Source LLC
Chambersburg PA
CBHW071534120626
46550CB00006B/2457